W9-BFZ-584

The Cabin

The Sound of Hard C

By Cynthia Amoroso and Bob Noyed

2

At the cabin, I wear my cap.

At the cabin, I call my cat.

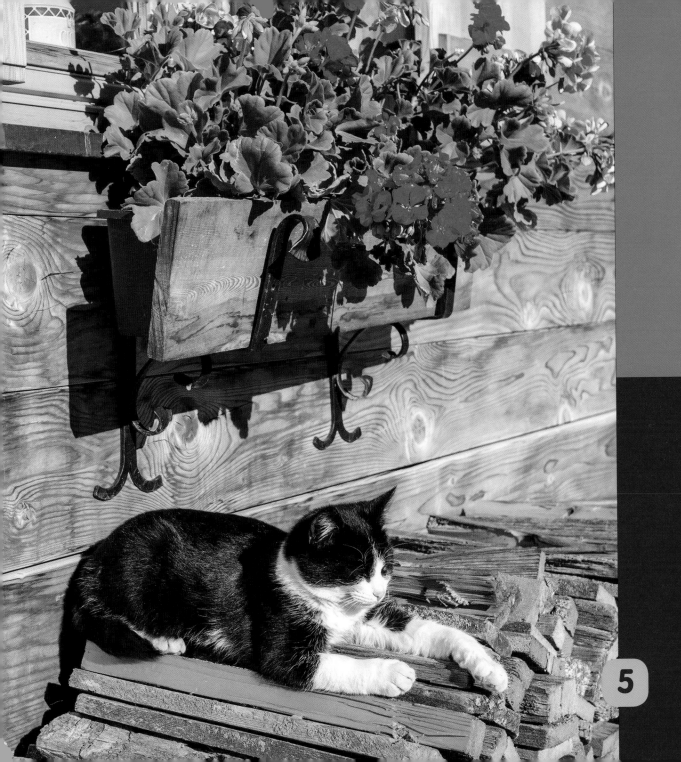

5

At the cabin, the lake is calm.

At the cabin,
I see the cub.

9

10

At the cabin, I hike to the cave.

At the cabin,
I drink from
my canteen.

13

At the cabin, the sun casts my shadow.

At the cabin, we cut wood for the fire.

17

At the cabin,
I drink cocoa
in my cup.

At the cabin,
I curl up to
take a catnap.

Word List:

cabin

calm

canteen

cap

casts

cat

catnap

cave

cocoa

cub

cup

curl

cut

Note to Parents and Educators

The books in this series are based on current research, which supports the idea that our brains are pattern-detectors rather than rules-appliers. This means children learn to read easier when they are taught the familiar spelling patterns found in English. As children encounter more complex words, they have greater success in figuring out these words by using the spelling patterns.

Throughout the series, the texts provide the reader with the opportunity to practice and apply knowledge of the sounds in natural language. The books introduce sounds using familiar onsets and *rimes*, or spelling patterns, for reinforcement.

For example, the word *cat* might be used to present the short "a" sound, with the letter *c* being the onset and "_at" being the rime. This approach provides practice and reinforcement of the short "a" sound, as there are many familiar words made with the "_at" rime.

The stories and accompanying photographs in this series are based on time-honored concepts in children's literature: well-written, engaging texts and colorful, high-quality photographs combine to produce books that children want to read again and again.

Dr. Peg Ballard
Minnesota State University, Mankato

The Child's World®

childsworld.com

Published by The Child's World®
1980 Lookout Drive • Mankato, MN 56003-1705
800-599-READ • www.childsworld.com

ACKNOWLEDGMENTS
The Child's World®: Mary Swensen, Publishing Director
The Design Lab: Design
Michael Miller: Editing

PHOTO CREDITS
© Blend Images/Shutterstock.com: 21; Christopher
Gardiner/Shutterstock.com: 6; David P. Smith/
Shutterstock.com: cover; jadimages/Shutterstock.com: 9;
Lungnhuadsamui/Shutterstock.com: 14; MyImages-Micha/
Shutterstock.com: 13; Nataly Moskovka/Shutterstock.com:
17; Pawel Kazmierczak/Shutterstock.com: 5; Remistudio/
Shutterstock.com: 2; SaraJo/Shutterstock.com: 10;
zhekoss/Shutterstock.com: 18

ISBN 9781503809147
LCCN 2015958470

Printed in the United States of America
Mankato, MN
June, 2016
PA02310

ABOUT THE AUTHORS

Cynthia Amoroso holds undergraduate
degrees in English and elementary educa-
tion, and graduate degrees in curriculum
and instruction as well as educational ad-
ministration. She is currently an assistant
superintendent in a suburban metropolitan
school district. Cynthia's past roles include
teacher, assistant principal, district reading
coordinator, director of curriculum and
instruction, and curriculum consultant.
She has extensive experience in reading,
literacy, curriculum development, pro-
fessional development, and continuous
improvement processes.

Bob Noyed started his career as a news-
paper reporter and freelance writer. Since
then, he has worked in school communica-
tions and public relations at the state and
national levels. He continues to write for
both children and adult audiences. Bob
lives in Woodbury, Minnesota.